"The Power of (

Written by Melvin Thomas III

"The Power of Oneness" is an exciting and informative novel that explores the history of spirituality and the importance of oneness in our lives. Each chapter takes the reader on a journey through the lives of different spiritual leaders, from Adam and Eve to Mirza Ghulam Ahmad, and explores how their teachings and experiences can help us connect with the source and achieve oneness.

What makes this novel so engaging is the author's passion for the subject matter. Each chapter is filled with vivid descriptions and powerful quotes that bring the teachings of these spiritual leaders to life. Whether it's the story of Noah and the flood or the teachings of Jesus on love and compassion, the author's enthusiasm for the subject matter is infectious and makes the book a joy to read.

But "The Power of Oneness" is more than just a fun read. It is also an informative and insightful exploration of the importance of spirituality in our lives. Through the stories of these spiritual leaders, the reader learns about the different practices and beliefs that can help us connect with the source and achieve oneness. Whether it's meditation, prayer, or connection with the chakras, the book offers practical advice on how we can align ourselves with the energy of oneness and live a more fulfilling life.

One of the most interesting aspects of the book is its exploration of the role of astrology in spirituality. From Abraham to Muhammad, many of the spiritual leaders featured in the book used astrology as a tool to understand the will of the source and to guide their people. The author does an excellent job of explaining the basics of astrology and how it can be used as a tool for spiritual growth.

Overall, "The Power of Oneness" is an excellent read for anyone interested in spirituality and the importance of oneness in our lives. With its passionate writing and insightful exploration of spiritual practices, the book is sure to inspire readers to connect with the source and live a life of oneness.

"One Source, One Love, One Power: Discovering the Power of Oneness"

I. Introduction
- The creation of the universe by a single source of energy
- The importance of astrology in understanding the will of the source
- The need for balance and alignment with the source through the chakras

II. Spiritual Leaders and their Teachings
- Adam and Eve and the story of the great flood
- Abraham and the use of astrology to guide his people
- Moses and the importance of oneness in the Ten Commandments

- David and the use of meditation and prayer to align himself with the source
- Elijah and the power of oneness to defeat false gods
- Isaiah and the importance of oneness and the coming of a messiah
- John the Baptist and the recognition of Jesus as the savior of humanity
- Jesus and the teachings of love and oneness
- Muhammad and the teachings of Islam
- Guru Nanak and the importance of meditation and devotion
- Baha'u'llah and the unity of all religions
- Mirza Ghulam Ahmad and the personal relationship with the source

III. The Importance of Spirituality in Our Lives
- Practical advice on how to connect with the source and achieve oneness
- The role of meditation, prayer, and connection with the chakras
- The role of astrology in understanding the will of the source

IV. Conclusion
- The future of spirituality and the promise of oneness
- The importance of choosing the path of oneness and seeking a closer relationship with the source.

Chapter 1: Creation and the Cosmos

In the beginning, before time and space, there was only a single source of energy. This energy was infinite, boundless, and omnipresent. The source was known by many names, including Yahweh, Allah, and Elohim, and it created all life on Earth, including Adam and Eve.

The source was the ultimate force of creation, the primordial essence that gave birth to the cosmos. It was the spark that ignited the Big Bang, the explosive event that brought the universe into existence. From that single moment, the cosmos began to expand and evolve, creating galaxies, stars, planets, and all the wondrous phenomena that make up the universe.

As the cosmos evolved, the source imbued it with a purpose, a reason for existence. The cosmos reflected the source's power and majesty, a testament to its infinite wisdom and creativity. Each aspect of the cosmos, from the smallest subatomic particle to the largest galaxy cluster, was a manifestation of the source's energy and intention.

The creation of the cosmos was a process that took billions of years. In the early stages, the universe was a hot, dense soup of particles that eventually cooled and coalesced into the first stars and galaxies. Over time, these stars exploded, scattering their atoms and elements throughout the cosmos, creating the building blocks for new stars, planets, and life.

The creation of human life was a pivotal moment in the history of the cosmos. Humans were a unique expression of the source's infinite creativity, imbued with a purpose and a reason for existence. Human life was a microcosm of the universe, a reflection of the same energy and intention that created the cosmos.

Astrology was the study of the influence of celestial bodies on human life. It was a tool that allowed humans to understand the deeper meaning behind the movements of the planets, stars, and galaxies. Astrology helped humans to align themselves with the source's intention and to understand their place in the cosmos.

Astronomy was also a tool that humans used to understand the cosmos. It was the study of the physical properties of the universe, from the properties of individual stars to the structure of the entire universe. Astronomy allowed humans to understand the mechanics of the cosmos and to appreciate the intricate balance of energy and matter that created the universe.

Human life was more than just a reflection of the cosmos. It was also an expression of the source's energy and intention. The chakras, or energy centers of the body, ere a reflection of the need for balance and alignment with the source. Each chakra was a reflection of a different aspect of the source's energy, from the root chakra, which represented stability and grounding, to the crown chakra, which represented spiritual connection and enlightenment.

The source imbued each human being with a purpose, a reason for existence that was unique and specific. It was up to each individual to find their purpose and to align themselves with the source's intention. This required a deep connection with the source, a spiritual journey that allowed humans to connect with the source's energy and to understand their place in the cosmos.

The cosmos and human life were a reflection of the same energy and intention that created the universe. The source was the ultimate force of creation, imbuing each aspect of the cosmos with a purpose and a reason for existence. Astrology, astronomy, and the chakras were all tools that humans used to understand the deeper meaning behind the universe and to align themselves with the source's intention. And ultimately, it was up to each individual to find their purpose and to connect with the source's energy, in order to live a life of oneness and to fulfill their true potential.

Chapter 2: The Flood and the Chakras

As humanity continued to grow and evolve, they began to lose sight of their connection to the source of all creation. They became consumed with their own desires and selfishness, and the world became a place of chaos and destruction. The source looked upon the world with a heavy heart, and decided that it was time to take drastic action.

The source sent a great flood to wipe out all life on Earth, except for Noah and his family. The flood was a warning to humanity that they must stay true to the path of oneness and reconnect with the source. The flood was also a symbol of purification, washing away the sins and corruption of humanity.

Noah and his family were chosen to survive the flood because they were righteous and lived a life of oneness. They understood the importance of staying connected to the source and living a life of balance and harmony.

When the flood came, they were prepared and were able to survive and rebuild the world.

The flood was a reminder to humanity that they must stay true to the path of oneness and live a life of balance and harmony. One way to achieve this balance is through the chakras, or energy centers of the body.

The chakras are a reflection of the need for balance and alignment with the source. There are seven major chakras in the body, each corresponding to a different area of life. The first chakra, known as the root chakra, is located at the base of the spine and is associated with survival and grounding. The second chakra, known as the sacral chakra, is located in the lower abdomen and is associated with creativity and sexuality. The third chakra, known as the solar plexus chakra, is located in the upper abdomen and is associated with personal power and self-esteem. The fourth chakra, known as the heart chakra, is located in the center of the chest and is associated with love and compassion. The fifth chakra, known as the throat chakra, is located in the throat and is associated with communication and self-expression. The sixth chakra, known as the third eye chakra, is located in the center of the forehead and is associated with intuition and spiritual insight. The seventh chakra, known as the crown chakra, is located at the top of the head and is associated with spiritual connection and enlightenment.

When the chakras are balanced and aligned, the individual is able to live a life of oneness and harmony. They are able to connect with the source and receive guidance and inspiration. However, when the chakras are blocked or unbalanced, the individual may experience physical, emotional, or spiritual distress.

We can use the flood as a metaphorical cleansing of the chakras, forcing humanity to purify and balance their energy centers in order to survive and thrive. It was a reminder that in order to live a life of oneness and connection to the source, we must first maintain balance and alignment within ourselves.

Overall, the flood and the chakras are both symbols of the need for balance and alignment. The flood was a warning to humanity to stay true to the path of oneness and to reconnect with the source. The chakras are a reflection of this need for balance and alignment within us. By maintaining balance and alignment within ourselves, we are able to connect with the source and live a life of oneness and harmony.

Chapter 3: Abraham and Astrology

Abraham was a righteous man who believed in the power of oneness. The source chose him to be the father of a great nation, and Abraham accepted this responsibility with humility and grace. He understood that he had been chosen for a special purpose, and he dedicated his life to serving the source and spreading the message of oneness,

As Abraham's fame and influence grew, he was tested by the source. He was asked to sacrifice his son, Isaac, as a test of his faith and obedience. Abraham was torn between his love for his son and his devotion to the source, but ultimately, he remained faithful and received the blessings of the source. His willingness to sacrifice his son was a symbol of his devotion to the source and his commitment to oneness. It was also a sign of his understanding that everything in the universe is interconnected, and that every action has consequences.

Astrology was a tool that Abraham used to understand the will of the source and to guide his people. He understood that the movements of the stars and planets were a reflection of the source's power and majesty, and he used this knowledge to gain insight into the source's plan for humanity. He also believed that the source had created the heavens and the earth, and that the movements of the celestial bodies were a sign of the source's power and will. He studied the stars and planets carefully, and he used this knowledge to guide his people in their daily lives.

Astrology was also a way for Abraham to connect with the source on a deeper level. By studying the movements of the stars and planets, he was able to gain insight into the source's plan for humanity and to understand his own place in the universe.

Abraham's unique use of astrology was a reflection of his belief in the interconnectedness of all things. He understood that every action has consequences, and that everything in the universe is part of a greater whole. By studying the movements of the stars and planets, he was able to gain a deeper understanding of this interconnectedness and to guide his people towards a life of oneness.

He was chosen by the source to be the father of a great nation, and he accepted this responsibility with humility and grace. His willingness to sacrifice his son was a symbol of his devotion to the source, and his use of astrology was a reflection of his belief in the interconnectedness of all things. Abraham's life and his legacy is a testament to the power of oneness and the interconnectedness of all things.

Chapter 4: Moses and Astronomy

Moses was a great prophet and leader who was chosen by the source to lead the Israelites out of slavery in Egypt. He was a man of great faith and wisdom, and he used his connection to the source to guide his people towards a life of oneness.

With the power of oneness, Moses was able to perform miracles that demonstrated the source's power and will. One of the most famous of these miracles was the parting of the Red Sea, which allowed the Israelites to escape from the pursuing Egyptian army.

He also understood that the source's power was available to him at all times, and he used this power to lead his people through the desert towards the promised land. He received the Ten Commandments from the source, which emphasized the importance of oneness and the need to stay connected to the source.

Astronomy was also a tool that Moses used to guide his people through the desert. He understood that the movements of the stars and planets were a sign of the source's will, and he used this knowledge to navigate through the desert and to understand the source's plan for his people.

He was a skilled astronomer who used his knowledge to guide his people towards the promised land. Understanding that the stars and planets were a reflection of the source's power and majesty, he used this knowledge to gain insight into the source's plan for his people.

By studying the movements of the stars and planets, Moses was able to navigate through the desert and to guide his people towards a life of oneness. He understood that everything in the universe was interconnected, and that every action had consequences.

His use of astronomy was a reflection of his belief in the interconnectedness of all things. He understood that every action had consequences, and that everything in the universe was part of a greater whole. By studying the movements of the stars and planets, he was able to gain a deeper understanding of this interconnectedness and to guide his people towards a life of oneness.

Moses used the power of oneness and the tools of astronomy to guide his people towards a life of oneness. He understood that the movements of the stars and planets were a reflection of the source's power and will, and he used this knowledge to navigate through the desert and to understand the source's plan for his people. His teachings continue to inspire people still to this day, and his legacy is a testament to the power of oneness and the interconnectedness of all things.

Chapter 5: David and Chakras

David was a great king who united the tribes of Israel and established a powerful kingdom. He was a man of oneness who wrote many psalms to praise the source and to express his devotion to oneness.

David, like many others, understood the importance of staying connected to the source, and he used his position as king to lead his people towards a life of oneness. He believed that the key to achieving oneness was through the chakras, or energy centers of the body. He used meditation and prayer to align himself with the source and to balance his chakras. He understood that when the chakras were balanced and aligned, the individual was able to live a life of oneness and connection to the source. His incredible devotion to oneness and his understanding of the chakras were reflected in his psalms. He wrote many psalms that praised the source and expressed his gratitude for the blessings that he had received.

David's use of the chakras was a reflection of his belief in the interconnectedness of all things. He understood that every action had consequences, and that everything in the universe was part of a greater whole. By balancing and aligning his chakras, he was able to connect with the source on a deeper level and to lead his people towards a life of oneness. David's bravery and devotion to oneness inspired his people and helped to establish a powerful kingdom that lasted for many years and his teachings on the importance of the chakras and oneness remain as relevant as ever.

He was a great king who understood the importance of oneness and the chakras. His use of meditation and prayer to balance and align his chakras reflected his belief in the interconnectedness of all things. His legacy continues to inspire people to this day, and his teachings on the importance of oneness and the chakras remain as relevant as ever.

Chapter 6: Elijah and Spirituality

Elijah was a prophet who lived during a time when the worship of false gods was prevalent. He challenged this worship and called upon the power of oneness to defeat the prophets of Baal. He understood the importance of connecting with the source and living a life of oneness. He believed that the source was the only true power, and that all other gods were false and misleading.

Elijah's victory over the prophets of Baal was a symbol of the power of oneness. He called upon the source to send down fire from heaven and to consume his sacrifice, demonstrating the source's power and will. Elijah's close relationship with the source was also demonstrated by his departure from this world. He was taken up to heaven in a whirlwind, a symbol of his closeness to the source and his faith in oneness.

Elijah understood the importance of connecting with the source and living a life of oneness. He believed that the source was the true power in the universe, and that all other gods were false and misleading. He understood that connecting with the source was the key to living a meaningful and fulfilling life, and he encouraged his followers to seek out this connection and to live a life of oneness.

Elijah was a prophet who challenged the worship of false gods and called upon the power of oneness to defeat the prophets of Baal. He was taken up to heaven in a whirlwind, a symbol of his closeness to the source. He was a spiritual leader who understood the importance of connecting with the source and living a life of oneness. His legacy is a hidden testament to the power of oneness and the importance of connecting with the source.

Chapter 7: Isaiah and Chakras

Isaiah was a prophet who lived in a time of great turmoil and uncertainty, and he spoke of the coming of a messiah who would bring humanity back to oneness. Isaiah emphasized the importance of oneness and righteousness, and he called for people to repent and return to the path of righteousness. His teachings were rooted in his understanding of the chakras, which were energy centers of the body that were essential for connecting with the source and living a life of oneness. Isaiah used meditation and prayer to align himself with the source and to receive divine messages, which led him to prophesy about the coming of a messiah.

Isaiah's understanding of the chakras was reflected in his prophecies, which foretold of a time when the source would send a savior to bring humanity back to oneness. His teachings on oneness, righteousness, and the chakras continue to inspire people to this day, and his legacy is a testament to the power of connecting with the source through the chakras. His teachings have been passed down from generation to generation. The message of the chakras is still relevant today, and people are discovering the benefits of aligning their chakras to connect with the source.

Isaiah teachings were rooted in his understanding of the chakras, which were essential for connecting with the source and living a life of oneness. Isaiah's legacy continues and his teachings on the chakras remain as relevant as ever. By aligning our chakras and connecting with the source, we can experience a deeper sense of connection and purpose in our lives.

Chapter 8: John the Baptist and Spirituality

John the Baptist was a prophet who prepared the way for the messiah. He was a spiritual leader who understood the importance of connecting with the source and living a life of oneness. John recognized Jesus as the savior who would bring humanity back to oneness, and he called for people to repent and be baptized in the name of oneness.

His message was based on his understanding of spirituality, which he saw as a way of connecting with the source and living a life of oneness. He believed that spirituality was not about following rules or rituals, but rather about cultivating a deep and meaningful connection with the source. For John, spirituality was about living a life of service and compassion. He saw himself as a servant of the source, and he dedicated his life to preparing the way for the messiah. He believed that by serving others and living a life of oneness, he was serving the source.

John's teachings on spirituality were reflected in his baptismal rituals. He saw baptism as a way of washing away the impurities of the ego and connecting with the source on a deeper level. His baptismal rituals were not just about the physical act of immersion; they were about the spiritual transformation that occurred as a result of immersion.

John's understanding of spirituality was also reflected in his ascetic lifestyle. He lived in the desert, wore simple clothing made of camel's hair, and ate locusts and honey! John's ascetic lifestyle was not just about self-denial; it was about cultivating a deep and meaningful connection with the source.

He understood that the key to living a meaningful and fulfilling life was to connect with the source on a deep and profound level. By living a life of service, compassion, and oneness, we can cultivate this connection and experience the beauty and wonder of the world around us.

John the Baptist knew the importance of connecting with the source and living a life of oneness. His teachings on spirituality and oneness were reflected in his baptismal rituals and ascetic lifestyle, and they continue to inspire people to this day. By living a life of service, compassion, and oneness, we can cultivate a deep and meaningful connection with the source and experience the beauty and wonder of the world around us.

Chapter 9: Jesus and Spirituality

Jesus is one of the most influential spiritual leaders in human history. His teachings and message of oneness have had a profound impact on countless people throughout the world. Jesus was the son of the source who came to Earth to bring humanity back to oneness. He taught that the source was within all people and that they could achieve oneness by loving one another.

His divine message of oneness was received by his understanding of spirituality. He saw spirituality as a way of connecting with the source and living a life of oneness. He believed that the key to living a meaningful and fulfilling life was to cultivate a deep and meaningful connection with the source.

For Jesus, spirituality was not just about following rules or rituals; it was about living a life of service and compassion. He saw himself as a servant of the source, and he dedicated his life to helping others and spreading the message of oneness. Jesus' teachings on spirituality were reflected in his life and his actions. He lived a life of oneness, and he taught others to do the same. He healed the sick, fed the hungry, and showed compassion and kindness to all people, regardless of their social status or background. Unfortunately, Jesus's message of oneness was not always well-received. He was crucified for his teachings, but his resurrection demonstrated the power of oneness over death. His message of oneness and love continues to inspire people to this day.

Jesus' teachings on spirituality and oneness have had a profound impact on countless people throughout history. His message of love and compassion has inspired people to live a life of service and to connect with the source on a deep and meaningful level.

His teachings on spirituality and oneness have had a profound impact on countless people throughout history. Jesus' message of love and compassion has inspired people to live a life of service and to connect with the source on a deep and meaningful level. By embracing his message of oneness and love, we can create a world that is filled with compassion, kindness, and peace.

Chapter 10: Muhammad and Astrology

Muhammad was a prophet who received the teachings of oneness from the source. He taught that there was only one God and that all people were equal in the eyes of oneness. His teachings formed the basis of Islam, a religion that emphasized the importance of oneness. Muhammad also used astrology to understand the will of the source and to guide his people.

Astrology has been used for centuries as a way of understanding the universe and our place in it. It is the study of the movements and relative positions of celestial bodies, and it has been used to predict the future, understand human behavior, and gain insight into the workings of the universe.

Muhammad was no stranger to astrology. He used it as a way of understanding the will of the source and guiding his people. Muhammad believed that the movements of the stars and planets were a reflection of the will of the source, and that by studying them, he could gain insight into the workings of the universe.

Muhammad's use of astrology was not limited to personal guidance. He also used it to make important decisions for his people. For example, when he was deciding where to build the mosque in Medina, he used astrology to determine the most auspicious location.

Muhammad's use of astrology was not just about predicting the future or making decisions. It was also about understanding the interconnectedness of all things. Muhammad believed that everything in the universe was connected, and that by studying the movements of the stars and planets, he could gain insight into the workings of the universe and the oneness of all things.

His message of oneness and equality is reflected in the teachings of Islam, and his use of astrology demonstrates the importance of understanding the interconnectedness of all things.

He taught that there was only one God and that all people were equal in the eyes of oneness. Muhammad used astrology as a way of understanding the will of the source and guiding his people. His teachings on oneness and astrology continue to inspire people to this day. By embracing his message of oneness and understanding the interconnectedness of all things, we can create a world that is filled with compassion, kindness, and peace.

Chapter 11: Guru Nanak and Chakras

Guru Nanak was a spiritual leader who founded Sikhism. He was born in the Punjab region of India in the 15th century and spent his life spreading the message of oneness and love. Guru Nanak taught that oneness could be achieved through meditation and devotion to the source. His teachings emphasized the importance of treating all people with respect and love. Guru Nanak also understood the importance of the chakras, using meditation and prayer to align himself with the source and to receive divine messages.

The chakras are energy centers located throughout the body, according to ancient Hindu and Buddhist traditions. These energy centers are believed to be responsible for various aspects of our physical, emotional, and spiritual well-being. Guru Nanak understood the importance of the chakras and used meditation and prayer to activate these energy centers and align himself with the source.

Each of the chakras is associated with a different aspect of our being. The root chakra, located at the base of the spine, is associated with our sense of security and grounding. The sacral chakra, located in the lower abdomen, is associated with our creativity and sexuality. The solar plexus chakra, located in the upper abdomen, is associated with our personal power and self-esteem. The heart chakra, located in the center of the chest, is associated with our ability to love and connect with others. The throat chakra, located in the throat, is associated with our ability to communicate and express ourselves. The third eye chakra, located in the center of the forehead, is associated with our intuition and spiritual awareness. The crown chakra, located at the top of the head, is associated with our connection to the source.

Guru Nanak used meditation and prayer to activate each of these chakras and align himself with the source. He understood that by aligning oneself with the source, one could achieve a state of oneness and connect with the divine.

He also believed in the importance of treating all people with respect and love. He taught that all people were equal in the eyes of the source, and that we should treat others as we would like to be treated. This message of love and equality is reflected in the teachings of Sikhism and continues to inspire people to this day.

He taught that oneness could be achieved through devotion to the source and that treating all people with respect and love was essential to achieving this state of oneness. Guru Nanak's teachings on the chakras and oneness continue to inspire people to this day, reminding us of the importance of spiritual connection and love for all beings.

Chapter 12: Baha'u'llah and Astrology

Baha'u'llah was a prophet who founded the Baha'i Faith in the 19th century. He taught that there was only one source who had sent messengers throughout history to guide humanity towards oneness. His teachings emphasized the importance of unity and the elimination of prejudice. Baha'u'llah also used astrology to understand the will of the source and to guide his people.

Astrology has been used for centuries as a way of understanding the universe and our place in it. It is the study of the movements and relative positions of celestial bodies, and it has been used to predict the future, understand human behavior, and gain insight into the workings of the universe.

Baha'u'llah understood the importance of astrology in gaining insight into the workings of the universe and the will of the source. He believed that the movements of the stars and planets were a reflection of the will of the source, and that by studying them, he could gain insight into the workings of the universe. His use of astrology was not limited to personal guidance. He also used it to make important decisions for his people. For example, when he was deciding where to establish the administrative center of the Baha'i Faith, he used astrology to determine the most auspicious location.

Baha'u'llah's use of astrology was not just about predicting the future or making decisions. It was also about understanding the interconnectedness of all things. Baha'u'llah believed that everything in the universe was connected, and that by studying the movements of the stars and planets, he could gain insight into the workings of the universe and the oneness of all things.

His teachings on oneness and unity continue to inspire people to this day. His message of unity and the elimination of prejudice is reflected in the teachings of the Baha'i Faith, and his use of astrology demonstrates the importance of understanding the interconnectedness of all things.

In addition to his teachings on oneness and astrology, Baha'u'llah also emphasized the importance of personal intuition and spiritual experience. He believed that each person had the ability to connect with the source and to receive divine guidance through their own intuition.

Baha'u'llah's teachings on personal intuition and spiritual experience remind us of the importance of trusting our own inner voice and connecting with the source on a deep and personal level. By embracing our intuition and spiritual experience, we can gain insight into the workings of the universe and our place in it.

He used astrology as a way of understanding the will of the source and guiding his people. Baha'u'llah's teachings on oneness, unity, and personal intuition continue to inspire people to this day, reminding us of the importance of understanding the interconnectedness of all things and trusting our own inner voice. By embracing these teachings, we can create a world that is filled with unity, love, and compassion.

Chapter 13: Mirza Ghulam Ahmad and Chakras

Mirza Ghulam Ahmad was born in Qadian, India. He founded the Ahmadiyya Muslim Community in the late 19th century and spent his life spreading the message of oneness and the importance of a personal relationship with the source. Mirza Ghulam Ahmad also understood the importance of the chakras, using meditation and prayer to align himself with the source and to receive divine messages.

Mirza Ghulam Ahmad's teachings on oneness centered around the idea of a personal relationship with the source. He believed that each person had the ability to connect with the source on a deep and personal level, and that this connection was essential to achieving a state of oneness. Mirza Ghulam Ahmad also taught that all people were equal in the eyes of oneness. He believed that no one person was better than another, and that each person had a unique and important role to play in the world. In addition to his teachings on oneness and equality, Mirza Ghulam Ahmad also understood the importance of the chakras. He believed that the chakras were energy centers located throughout the body, and that they were responsible for various aspects of our physical, emotional, and spiritual well-being.

Mirza Ghulam Ahmad used meditation and prayer to activate these chakras and align himself with the source. He believed that by doing so, he could receive divine messages and guidance.

One example of his use of the chakras can be found in his book, "The Philosophy of the Teachings of Islam." In this book, he describes the chakras in detail and explains how they can be activated through meditation and prayer.

Mirza Ghulam Ahmad also believed in the importance of personal intuition and spiritual experience. He believed that each person had the ability to connect with the source on a deep and personal level, and that this connection could be achieved through meditation, prayer, and other spiritual practices.

His emphasis on a personal relationship with the source and the importance of personal intuition and spiritual experience remind us of the importance of connecting with the source on a deep and personal level.

He taught that oneness could be achieved through a personal relationship with the source, and that all people were equal in the eyes of oneness. Mirza Ghulam Ahmad also understood the importance of the chakras, using meditation and prayer to align himself with the source and to receive divine messages. His teachings continue to inspire people to this day, reminding us of the importance of spiritual connection, personal intuition, and living a life of love and compassion.

Chapter 14: The Future and Spirituality

The future holds great promise for those who seek oneness. The source continues to send messengers to guide humanity towards oneness. It is up to everyone to choose the path of oneness and to seek a closer relationship with the source. Spirituality, through practices like meditation, prayer, and connection with the chakras, can help individuals to align themselves with the source and to live a life of oneness.

Throughout history, the source has sent messengers to guide humanity towards oneness. These messengers have included prophets, teachers, and spiritual leaders, each with their own unique message and teachings. These messengers have included figures such as Jesus Christ, Buddha, Muhammad, and many others.

Each of these messengers has taught a message of oneness and the importance of connecting with the source. They have taught that the source is the ultimate reality and that all things are connected. They have emphasized the importance of love, compassion, and service, and they have taught that each person has the ability to connect with the source on a deep and personal level.

As we move into the future, it is up to each individual to choose the path of oneness and to seek a closer relationship with the source. This can be done through practices like meditation, prayer, and connection with the chakras.

Meditation is a powerful tool for connecting with the source and aligning oneself with the energy of oneness. Through meditation, we can quiet the mind and open ourselves up to the energy of the universe. We can connect with the source on a deep and personal level, gaining insight into the workings of the universe and our place in it.

Prayer is another powerful tool for connecting with the source. Through prayer, we can express our gratitude, ask for guidance, and connect with the energy of oneness. We can ask for help in achieving our goals and living a life of love and compassion.

Connection with the chakras is also important for aligning oneself with the source. The chakras are energy centers located throughout the body, and they are responsible for various aspects of our physical, emotional, and spiritual well-being. By activating these chakras through meditation and prayer, we can align ourselves with the source and gain insight into the workings of the universe.

As we move into the future, it is important to remember that spirituality is an ongoing journey. It is not something that can be achieved overnight, but rather a lifelong process of growth and self-discovery. It is up to each individual to choose the path of oneness and to seek a closer relationship with the source.

In the words of Rumi, a 13th-century Persian poet and mystic, "The garden of the world has no limits, except in your mind. Its presence is more beautiful than the stars with more clarity than the polished mirror. The world's greatest art is not to know what to do but to be."

The future holds great promise for those who choose the path of oneness and seek a closer relationship with the source. As we continue on our spiritual journey, we can find peace, love, and compassion, and we can work towards creating a world that is filled with unity, love, and oneness.

Printed in Great Britain
by Amazon